My Feet Do

by Jean Holzenthaler
photographs by George Ancona

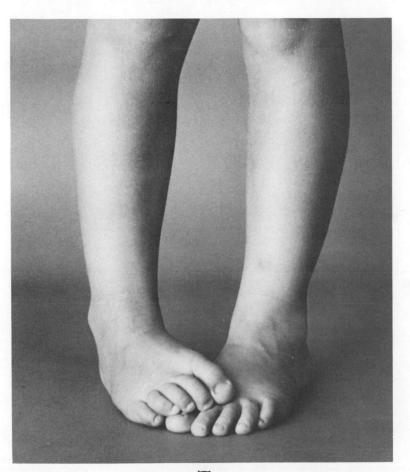

A Fat Cat Book
E. P. DUTTON   NEW YORK

To Nancy
J.H.

To Corina
G.A.

Library of Congress Cataloging in Publication Data

Holzenthaler, Jean.   My feet do.
(A Fat cat book)

SUMMARY: Describes the many things one's feet can do.
[1. Foot]   I. Ancona, George.   II. Title.   III. Series.
PZ7.H7436Mw   [E]   78-13143   ISBN: 0-525-35485-9

Published in the United States by E. P. Dutton, a Division
of Sequoia-Elsevier Publishing Company, Inc., New York

Published simultaneously in Canada by Clarke,
Irwin & Company Limited, Toronto and Vancouver

Editor: Ann Troy   Designer: Riki Levinson

Printed in the U.S.A.   First Edition
10 9 8 7 6 5 4 3 2 1

I have two feet.

This is my left foot.

This is my right foot.

My feet can do many things.

Kick.

Splash.

Jump.

Skip.

Walk.

Run.

And trip.

Feet that trip
can make me cry.

My feet make tracks
in snow.

They dance on tiptoe.

My feet can make me laugh.

My feet wear skates
on the ice.

They wear sneakers
for play.

Boots keep them warm
and dry.

So do socks.

I can stand on both feet,

or on one at a time.

I have two busy feet.
They need a rest.

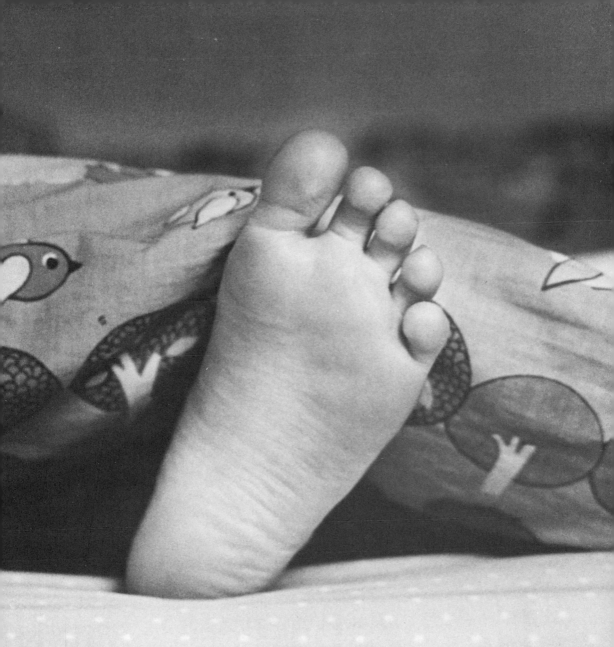

Now I like bare feet best.